This journal belongs to:

....

....

ISBN: 9798604128787

Recovery is a process.
It takes time and patience.
And most importantly a support system
from people around you.
People who
really, really, really
care about you.

"When everything seems like an uphill struggle,
just think of the view from the top."
– Unknown

Ideas for your daily affirmations

 I am grateful to be alive today!

 I am better today than yesterday

 Every new day is a blessing

 I forgive myself

 It's okay to make mistakes. Learn from it and get better

 I can be anything I want to be. I have a choice

 I accept for who I am

 I can make a difference

 I am responsible for who I am

 No one can change me but myself

Date _____

Day

I feel _____ this morning

Today's affirmation is _____

My ONE goal for today is _____

Accomplished? YES/NO

What can I do to make it better? _____

_____

Today, I ate : a little/ enough/ too much

I happily drink : 🥛🥛🥛🥛🥛🥛🥛

What I did today

☐ Take My Shower   ☐ Exercise   ☐ Prayers

☐ Outdoor Activities   ☐ _____   ☐ _____

AT NIGHT

Today, I am grateful for _____

My mood today : ☆ ☆ ☆ ☆ ☆

Did I stay sober today?   YES / NO

My thoughts for today

_____

_____

_____

> Yesterday is gone and its tale told. Today new seeds are growing - Rumi

Reflect .... Doodling .... Drawing ....

Date _____   *Day*

I feel _____ this morning

Today's affirmation is _____

My ONE goal for today is _____

Accomplished? YES/NO

What can I do to make it better? ————————————————

_____

Today, I ate : a little/ enough/ too much

I happily drink : 🥛🥛🥛🥛🥛🥛🥛

What I did today

☐ Take My Shower   ☐ Exercise   ☐ Prayers

☐ Outdoor Activities   ☐ _____   ☐ _____

AT NIGHT

Today, I am grateful for _____

My mood today : ☆ ☆ ☆ ☆ ☆

Did I stay sober today?   YES / NO

My thoughts for today

_____

_____

_____

“ To forgive is the highest, most
beautiful form of love.
In return, you will receive untold
peace and happiness.
- Robert Muller ”

Date _____  Day

I feel _____ this morning

Today's affirmation is _____

My ONE goal for today is _____

Accomplished? YES/NO

What can I do to make it better? _____

_____

Today, I ate : a little/ enough/ too much

I happily drink : 🥤🥤🥤🥤🥤🥤🥤

What I did today

☐ Take My Shower   ☐ Exercise   ☐ Prayers

☐ Outdoor Activities   ☐ _____   ☐ _____

AT NIGHT

Today, I am grateful for _____

My mood today : ☆ ☆ ☆ ☆ ☆

Did I stay sober today? YES / NO

My thoughts for today

_____

_____

_____

> **Our greatest glory is not in never failing, but in rising up every time we fail.**
> — Ralph Waldo Emerson

....

....

....

....

....

....

....

....

....

....

....

....

....

....

....

....

....

Date _____

Day

I feel _____ this morning

Today's affirmation is _____

My ONE goal for today is _____

Accomplished? YES/NO

What can I do to make it better? —————————————————

_____

Today, I ate : a little/ enough/ too much

I happily drink : ▯▯▯▯▯▯▯

What I did today

☐ Take My Shower   ☐ Exercise   ☐ Prayers

☐ Outdoor Activities   ☐ _____   ☐ _____

AT NIGHT

Today, I am grateful for _____

My mood today : ☆ ☆ ☆ ☆ ☆

Did I stay sober today?   YES / NO

My thoughts for today

_____

_____

_____

" Joy does not simply happen to us. We have to choose joy and keep choosing it every day.
 - Henri Nouwen **"**

Date _____

I feel _____ this morning

Today's affirmation is _____

My ONE goal for today is _____

Accomplished? YES/NO

What can I do to make it better? _____

_____

Today, I ate : a little/ enough/ too much

I happily drink : 🥛🥛🥛🥛🥛🥛🥛

What I did today

☐ Take My Shower   ☐ Exercise   ☐ Prayers

☐ Outdoor Activities ☐ _____   ☐ _____

AT NIGHT

Today, I am grateful for _____

My mood today : ☆ ☆ ☆ ☆ ☆

Did I stay sober today?   YES / NO

My thoughts for today

_____

_____

_____

66 Adopt the pace of nature; her
      secret is patience .
      - Ralph Waldo Enerson   99

....

....

....

....

....

....

....

....

....

....

....

....

....

....

....

....

....

....

Date _____

Day

I feel _____ this morning

Today's affirmation is _____

My ONE goal for today is _____

Accomplished? YES/NO

What can I do to make it better? ―――――――――――――

_____

Today, I ate : a little/ enough/ too much

I happily drink : 🥛🥛🥛🥛🥛🥛🥛

What I did today

☐ Take My Shower   ☐ Exercise   ☐ Prayers

☐ Outdoor Activities   ☐ _____   ☐ _____

AT NIGHT

Today, I am grateful for _____

My mood today : ☆ ☆ ☆ ☆ ☆

Did I stay sober today?   YES / NO

My thoughts for today

_____

_____

_____

*No one can make you feel
inferior without your consent.*
       - Eleanor Roosevelt

Reflect .... Doodling .... Drawing ...

Date _____

I feel _____ this morning

Today's affirmation is _____

My ONE goal for today is _____

Accomplished? YES/NO

What can I do to make it better? ——————————————————

_____

Today, I ate : a little/ enough/ too much

I happily drink : ▯▯▯▯▯▯▯

What I did today

☐ Take My Shower   ☐ Exercise   ☐ Prayers

☐ Outdoor Activities   ☐ _____   ☐ _____

AT NIGHT

Today, I am grateful for _____

My mood today : ☆ ☆ ☆ ☆ ☆

Did I stay sober today?   YES / NO

My thoughts for today

_____

_____

_____

Life often teaches us through
our wrong turns and missed
possibilities.
- Anne Wilson Schaef

Reflect .... Doodling ...... Drawing ...

Date _____

Day

I feel _____ this morning

Today's affirmation is _____

My ONE goal for today is _____

Accomplished? YES/NO

What can I do to make it better? _____
_____

Today, I ate : a little/ enough/ too much

I happily drink : ▢ ▢ ▢ ▢ ▢ ▢ ▢ ▢

What I did today

☐ Take My Shower   ☐ Exercise   ☐ Prayers

☐ Outdoor Activities ☐ _____   ☐ _____

AT NIGHT

Today, I am grateful for _____

My mood today : ☆ ☆ ☆ ☆ ☆

Did I stay sober today?   YES / NO

My thoughts for today

_____

_____

_____

It does not matter how
slowly you go as long as
you do not stop.
- Confucius

Reflect .... Doodling .... Drawing ....

Date _____  Day

I feel _____ this morning

Today's affirmation is _____

My ONE goal for today is _____

Accomplished? YES/NO

What can I do to make it better? _____

_____

Today, I ate : a little/ enough/ too much

I happily drink : 🥛🥛🥛🥛🥛🥛🥛

What I did today

☐ Take My Shower   ☐ Exercise   ☐ Prayers

☐ Outdoor Activities   ☐ _____   ☐ _____

AT NIGHT

Today, I am grateful for _____

My mood today : ☆ ☆ ☆ ☆ ☆

Did I stay sober today?   YES / NO

My thoughts for today

_____

_____

_____

" Learn from yesterday, live for
today, hope for tomorrow.
                - Albert Einstein   "

Date _____    Day

I feel _____ this morning

Today's affirmation is _____

My ONE goal for today is _____

Accomplished? YES/NO

What can I do to make it better? ————————————————

_____

Today, I ate : a little/ enough/ too much

I happily drink : 🥛🥛🥛🥛🥛🥛🥛

What I did today

☐ Take My Shower   ☐ Exercise   ☐ Prayers
☐ Outdoor Activities ☐ _____   ☐ _____

AT NIGHT

Today, I am grateful for _____

My mood today : ☆ ☆ ☆ ☆ ☆

Did I stay sober today?   YES / NO

My thoughts for today

_____
_____
_____

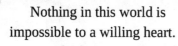

Nothing in this world is
impossible to a willing heart.
- Abraham Lincoln

Reflect .... Doodling .... Drawing ...

Date _____  Day

I feel _____ this morning

Today's affirmation is _____

My ONE goal for today is _____

Accomplished? YES/NO

What can I do to make it better? _____

_____

Today, I ate : a little/ enough/ too much

I happily drink : 🥛🥛🥛🥛🥛🥛🥛

What I did today

☐ Take My Shower   ☐ Exercise   ☐ Prayers

☐ Outdoor Activities   ☐ _____   ☐ _____

AT NIGHT

Today, I am grateful for _____

My mood today : ☆ ☆ ☆ ☆ ☆

Did I stay sober today?   YES / NO

My thoughts for today

_____

_____

_____

Everything gets better with time.
                    - Unknown

Date _____    Day

I feel _____ this morning

Today's affirmation is _____

My ONE goal for today is _____

Accomplished? YES/NO

What can I do to make it better? _____

_____

Today, I ate : a little/ enough/ too much

I happily drink : ▦ ▦ ▦ ▦ ▦ ▦ ▦

What I did today

☐ Take My Shower   ☐ Exercise   ☐ Prayers

☐ Outdoor Activities ☐ _____   ☐ _____

AT NIGHT

Today, I am grateful for _____

My mood today : ☆ ☆ ☆ ☆ ☆

Did I stay sober today?   YES / NO

My thoughts for today

_____

_____

_____

❝ When you forgive, you heal.
When you let go, you grow.
     - Anonymous   **❞**

Reflect .... Doodling ...... Drawing ...

Date _____

I feel _____ this morning

Today's affirmation is _____

My ONE goal for today is _____

Accomplished? YES/NO

What can I do to make it better? ————————————————

_____

Today, I ate : a little/ enough/ too much

I happily drink : ⊟⊟⊟⊟⊟⊟⊟

What I did today

☐ Take My Shower   ☐ Exercise   ☐ Prayers

☐ Outdoor Activities   ☐ _____   ☐ _____

AT NIGHT

Today, I am grateful for _____

My mood today : ☆ ☆ ☆ ☆ ☆

Did I stay sober today?   YES / NO

My thoughts for today

_____

_____

_____

❝ Yesterday is gone and its tale
told. Today new seeds are
growing - Rumi **❞**

Date _____

Day

I feel _____ this morning

Today's affirmation is _____

My ONE goal for today is _____

Accomplished? YES/NO

What can I do to make it better? ————————————

_____

Today, I ate : a little/ enough/ too much

I happily drink : 🥛🥛🥛🥛🥛🥛🥛

What I did today

☐ Take My Shower   ☐ Exercise   ☐ Prayers

☐ Outdoor Activities   ☐ _____   ☐ _____

AT NIGHT

Today, I am grateful for _____

My mood today : ☆ ☆ ☆ ☆ ☆

Did I stay sober today?   YES / NO

My thoughts for today

_____

_____

_____

To forgive is the highest, most
beautiful form of love.
In return, you will receive untold
peace and happiness.
- Robert Muller

Reflect .... Doodling .... Drawing ....

Date _____

I feel _____ this morning

Today's affirmation is _____

My ONE goal for today is _____

Accomplished? YES/NO

What can I do to make it better? ————————————————

_____

Today, I ate : a little/ enough/ too much

I happily drink : 🥛🥛🥛🥛🥛🥛🥛

What I did today

☐ Take My Shower   ☐ Exercise   ☐ Prayers

☐ Outdoor Activities   ☐ _____   ☐ _____

AT NIGHT

Today, I am grateful for _____

My mood today : ☆ ☆ ☆ ☆ ☆

Did I stay sober today?   YES / NO

My thoughts for today

_____

_____

_____

“ Our greatest glory is not in never
failing, but in rising up every
time we fail.
- Ralph Waldo Emerson ”

....

....

....

....

....

....

....

....

....

....

....

....

....

....

....

....

....

Reflect .... Doodling .... Drawing ....

Date _____

Day

I feel _____ this morning

Today's affirmation is _____

My ONE goal for today is _____

Accomplished? YES/NO

What can I do to make it better? ——————————————

_____

Today, I ate : a little/ enough/ too much

I happily drink : ▯ ▯ ▯ ▯ ▯ ▯ ▯ ▯

What I did today

☐ Take My Shower   ☐ Exercise   ☐ Prayers

☐ Outdoor Activities   ☐ _____   ☐ _____

AT NIGHT

Today, I am grateful for _____

My mood today : ☆ ☆ ☆ ☆ ☆

Did I stay sober today?   YES / NO

My thoughts for today

_____

_____

_____

Joy does not simply happen to us. We have to choose joy and keep choosing it every day.
- Henri Nouwen

Reflect .... Doodling ...... Drawing ...

Date _____

 Day

I feel _____ this morning

Today's affirmation is _____

My ONE goal for today is _____

Accomplished? YES/NO

What can I do to make it better? ——————————————

_____

Today, I ate : a little/ enough/ too much

I happily drink : 🥛🥛🥛🥛🥛🥛🥛🥛

What I did today

☐ Take My Shower   ☐ Exercise   ☐ Prayers

☐ Outdoor Activities ☐ _____   ☐ _____

AT NIGHT

Today, I am grateful for _____

My mood today : ☆ ☆ ☆ ☆ ☆

Did I stay sober today?   YES / NO

My thoughts for today

_____

_____

_____

Adopt the pace of nature; her
secret is patience .
- Ralph Waldo Enerson

Reflect .... Doodling ...... Drawing ....

Date _____    Day

I feel _____ this morning

Today's affirmation is _____

My ONE goal for today is _____

Accomplished? YES/NO

What can I do to make it better? ——————————————

_____

Today, I ate : a little/ enough/ too much

I happily drink : ⊞⊞⊞⊞⊞⊞⊞

What I did today

☐ Take My Shower   ☐ Exercise   ☐ Prayers

☐ Outdoor Activities   ☐ _____   ☐ _____

AT NIGHT

Today, I am grateful for _____

My mood today : ☆ ☆ ☆ ☆ ☆

Did I stay sober today?   YES / NO

My thoughts for today

_____

_____

_____

"

No one can make you feel
inferior without your consent.
- Eleanor Roosevelt "

Reflect .... Doodling .... Drawing ....

Date _____

Day

I feel _____ this morning

Today's affirmation is _____

My ONE goal for today is _____

Accomplished? YES/NO

What can I do to make it better? ————————————————
_____

Today, I ate : a little/ enough/ too much

I happily drink : ▢▢▢▢▢▢▢

What I did today

☐ Take My Shower   ☐ Exercise   ☐ Prayers

☐ Outdoor Activities ☐ _____   ☐ _____

AT NIGHT

Today, I am grateful for _____

My mood today : ☆ ☆ ☆ ☆ ☆

Did I stay sober today?   YES / NO

My thoughts for today

_____

_____

_____

" Life often teaches us through
our wrong turns and missed
possibilities.
- Anne Wilson Schaef **"**

Reflect .... Doodling ...... Drawing ...

Date _____

Day

I feel _____ this morning

Today's affirmation is _____

My ONE goal for today is _____

Accomplished? YES/NO

What can I do to make it better? ————————————————

_____

Today, I ate : a little/ enough/ too much

I happily drink : ▢▢▢▢▢▢▢

What I did today

☐ Take My Shower   ☐ Exercise   ☐ Prayers

☐ Outdoor Activities ☐ _____   ☐ _____

AT NIGHT

Today, I am grateful for _____

My mood today : ☆ ☆ ☆ ☆ ☆

Did I stay sober today?   YES / NO

My thoughts for today

_____

_____

_____

It does not matter how
slowly you go as long as
you do not stop.
- Confucius

Reflect .... Doodling ...... Drawing ...

Date _____

Day

I feel _____ this morning

Today's affirmation is _____

My ONE goal for today is _____

Accomplished? YES/NO

What can I do to make it better? _____

_____

Today, I ate : a little/ enough/ too much

I happily drink : 🥛🥛🥛🥛🥛🥛🥛

What I did today

☐ Take My Shower   ☐ Exercise   ☐ Prayers

☐ Outdoor Activities   ☐ _____   ☐ _____

AT NIGHT

Today, I am grateful for _____

My mood today : ☆ ☆ ☆ ☆ ☆

Did I stay sober today?   YES / NO

My thoughts for today

_____

_____

_____

66 Learn from yesterday, live for
today, hope for tomorrow.
- Albert Einstein 99

Date _____

Day

I feel _____ this morning

Today's affirmation is _____

My ONE goal for today is _____

Accomplished? YES/NO

What can I do to make it better? ─────────────────

_____

Today, I ate : a little/ enough/ too much

I happily drink : 🥤🥤🥤🥤🥤🥤🥤

What I did today

☐ Take My Shower   ☐ Exercise   ☐ Prayers

☐ Outdoor Activities   ☐ _____   ☐ _____

AT NIGHT

Today, I am grateful for _____

My mood today : ☆ ☆ ☆ ☆ ☆

Did I stay sober today?   YES / NO

My thoughts for today

_____

_____

_____

" Nothing in this world is
impossible to a willing heart.
  - Abraham Lincoln **"**

Reflect .... Doodling .... Drawing ....

Date _____    Day

I feel _____ this morning

Today's affirmation is _____

My ONE goal for today is _____

Accomplished? YES/NO

What can I do to make it better? —————————————

_____

Today, I ate : a little/ enough/ too much

I happily drink : 🥛🥛🥛🥛🥛🥛🥛

What I did today

☐ Take My Shower   ☐ Exercise   ☐ Prayers

☐ Outdoor Activities   ☐ _____   ☐ _____

AT NIGHT

Today, I am grateful for _____

My mood today : ☆ ☆ ☆ ☆ ☆

Did I stay sober today?   YES / NO

My thoughts for today

_____

_____

_____

" Everything gets better with time.
          - Unknown   "

(none)

Reflect .... Doodling .... Drawing ...

Date _____

 Day

I feel _____ this morning

Today's affirmation is _____

My ONE goal for today is _____

Accomplished? YES/NO

What can I do to make it better? —————————————

_____

Today, I ate : a little/ enough/ too much

I happily drink : 🥛🥛🥛🥛🥛🥛🥛

What I did today

☐ Take My Shower   ☐ Exercise   ☐ Prayers

☐ Outdoor Activities   ☐ _____   ☐ _____

AT NIGHT

Today, I am grateful for _____

My mood today : ☆ ☆ ☆ ☆ ☆

Did I stay sober today?   YES / NO

My thoughts for today

_____

_____

_____

"
When you forgive, you heal.
When you let go, you grow.
- Anonymous
"

Reflect .... Doodling .... Drawing ....

Date _____

Day

I feel _____ this morning

Today's affirmation is _____

My ONE goal for today is _____

Accomplished? YES/NO

What can I do to make it better? _____

_____

Today, I ate : a little/ enough/ too much

I happily drink : 🥛🥛🥛🥛🥛🥛🥛

What I did today

☐ Take My Shower   ☐ Exercise   ☐ Prayers

☐ Outdoor Activities   ☐ _____   ☐ _____

AT NIGHT

Today, I am grateful for _____

My mood today : ☆ ☆ ☆ ☆ ☆

Did I stay sober today?   YES / NO

My thoughts for today

_____

_____

_____

> Yesterday is gone and its tale told. Today new seeds are growing - Rumi "

....

....

....

....

....

....

....

....

....

....

....

....

....

....

....

....

....

Date _____    Day

I feel _____ this morning

Today's affirmation is _____

My ONE goal for today is _____

Accomplished? YES/NO

What can I do to make it better? ——————————————————

_____

Today, I ate : a little/ enough/ too much

I happily drink : 🥛🥛🥛🥛🥛🥛🥛

What I did today

☐ Take My Shower   ☐ Exercise   ☐ Prayers

☐ Outdoor Activities ☐ _____   ☐ _____

AT NIGHT

Today, I am grateful for _____

My mood today : ☆ ☆ ☆ ☆ ☆

Did I stay sober today?   YES / NO

My thoughts for today

_____

_____

_____

To forgive is the highest, most
beautiful form of love.
In return, you will receive untold
peace and happiness.
- Robert Muller

Reflect .... Doodling ...... Drawing ...

Date _____  Day

I feel _____ this morning

Today's affirmation is _____

My ONE goal for today is _____

Accomplished? YES/NO

What can I do to make it better? _____

_____

Today, I ate : a little/ enough/ too much

I happily drink : 🥃🥃🥃🥃🥃🥃🥃

What I did today

☐ Take My Shower   ☐ Exercise   ☐ Prayers

☐ Outdoor Activities   ☐ _____   ☐ _____

AT NIGHT

Today, I am grateful for _____

My mood today : ☆ ☆ ☆ ☆ ☆

Did I stay sober today?   YES / NO

My thoughts for today

_____

_____

_____

" Our greatest glory is not in never
failing, but in rising up every
time we fail.
- Ralph Waldo Emerson **"**

Date _____

Day

I feel _____ this morning

Today's affirmation is _____

My ONE goal for today is _____

Accomplished? YES/NO

What can I do to make it better? ——————————————

_____

Today, I ate : a little/ enough/ too much

I happily drink : 🥛🥛🥛🥛🥛🥛🥛

What I did today

☐ Take My Shower   ☐ Exercise   ☐ Prayers

☐ Outdoor Activities ☐ _____   ☐ _____

AT NIGHT

Today, I am grateful for _____

My mood today : ☆ ☆ ☆ ☆ ☆

Did I stay sober today?   YES / NO

My thoughts for today

_____

_____

_____

❝ Joy does not simply happen to
us. We have to choose joy and
keep choosing it every day.
- Henri Nouwen **❞**

Reflect .... Doodling .... Drawing ....

Date _____    Day

I feel _____ this morning

Today's affirmation is _____

My ONE goal for today is _____

Accomplished? YES/NO

What can I do to make it better? _____

_____

Today, I ate : a little/ enough/ too much

I happily drink : ⊡ ⊡ ⊡ ⊡ ⊡ ⊡ ⊡

What I did today

☐ Take My Shower   ☐ Exercise   ☐ Prayers

☐ Outdoor Activities   ☐ _____   ☐ _____

AT NIGHT

Today, I am grateful for _____

My mood today : ☆ ☆ ☆ ☆ ☆

Did I stay sober today?   YES / NO

My thoughts for today

_____

_____

_____

❝ Adopt the pace of nature; her
secret is patience .
- Ralph Waldo Enerson **❞**

....

....

....

....

....

....

....

....

....

....

....

....

....

....

....

....

....

....

Date _____    Day

I feel _____ this morning

Today's affirmation is _____

My ONE goal for today is _____

Accomplished? YES/NO

What can I do to make it better? ─────────────────────

_____

Today, I ate : a little/ enough/ too much

I happily drink : 🥛🥛🥛🥛🥛🥛🥛

What I did today

☐ Take My Shower   ☐ Exercise   ☐ Prayers

☐ Outdoor Activities   ☐ _____   ☐ _____

AT NIGHT

Today, I am grateful for _____

My mood today : ☆ ☆ ☆ ☆ ☆

Did I stay sober today?   YES / NO

My thoughts for today

_____

_____

_____

❝ No one can make you feel
inferior without your consent.
        - Eleanor Roosevelt   **❞**

Date _____

Day

I feel _____ this morning

Today's affirmation is _____

My ONE goal for today is _____

Accomplished? YES/NO

What can I do to make it better? ─────────────────

_____

Today, I ate : a little/ enough/ too much

I happily drink : 🥛🥛🥛🥛🥛🥛🥛

What I did today

☐ Take My Shower   ☐ Exercise   ☐ Prayers

☐ Outdoor Activities   ☐ _____   ☐ _____

AT NIGHT

Today, I am grateful for _____

My mood today : ☆ ☆ ☆ ☆ ☆

Did I stay sober today?   YES / NO

My thoughts for today

_____

_____

_____

❝ Life often teaches us through
our wrong turns and missed
possibilities.
- Anne Wilson Schaef ❞

Date _____

I feel _____ this morning

Today's affirmation is _____

My ONE goal for today is _____

Accomplished? YES/NO

What can I do to make it better? ────────────────────

_____

Today, I ate : a little/ enough/ too much

I happily drink : ▢▢▢▢▢▢▢

What I did today

☐ Take My Shower   ☐ Exercise   ☐ Prayers

☐ Outdoor Activities ☐ _____ ☐ _____

AT NIGHT

Today, I am grateful for _____

My mood today : ☆ ☆ ☆ ☆ ☆

Did I stay sober today?   YES / NO

My thoughts for today

_____

_____

_____

" It does not matter how
slowly you go as long as
you do not stop.
- Confucius "

Reflect .... Doodling .... Drawing ...

Date _____

Day

I feel _____ this morning

Today's affirmation is _____

My ONE goal for today is _____

Accomplished? YES/NO

What can I do to make it better? ——————————————————

_____

Today, I ate : a little/ enough/ too much

I happily drink : ▯▯▯▯▯▯▯

What I did today

☐ Take My Shower   ☐ Exercise   ☐ Prayers

☐ Outdoor Activities   ☐ _____   ☐ _____

AT NIGHT

Today, I am grateful for _____

My mood today : ☆ ☆ ☆ ☆ ☆

Did I stay sober today?   YES / NO

My thoughts for today

_____

_____

_____

“ Learn from yesterday, live for
today, hope for tomorrow.
   - Albert Einstein   **99**

Date _____

Day

I feel _____ this morning

Today's affirmation is _____

My ONE goal for today is _____

Accomplished? YES/NO

What can I do to make it better? ————————————————

_____

Today, I ate : a little/ enough/ too much

I happily drink : 🥛🥛🥛🥛🥛🥛🥛

What I did today

☐ Take My Shower   ☐ Exercise   ☐ Prayers

☐ Outdoor Activities ☐ _____ ☐ _____

AT NIGHT

Today, I am grateful for _____

My mood today : ☆ ☆ ☆ ☆ ☆

Did I stay sober today?   YES / NO

My thoughts for today

_____

_____

_____

" Nothing in this world is
impossible to a willing heart.
- Abraham Lincoln "

Reflect .... Doodling .... Drawing ....

Date _____

Day

I feel _____ this morning

Today's affirmation is _____

My ONE goal for today is _____

Accomplished? YES/NO

What can I do to make it better? _____

_____

Today, I ate : a little/ enough/ too much

I happily drink : 🥛🥛🥛🥛🥛🥛🥛

What I did today

☐ Take My Shower   ☐ Exercise   ☐ Prayers

☐ Outdoor Activities   ☐ _____   ☐ _____

AT NIGHT

Today, I am grateful for _____

My mood today : ☆ ☆ ☆ ☆ ☆

Did I stay sober today?   YES / NO

My thoughts for today

_____

_____

_____

Everything gets better with time.
- Unknown

Reflect .... Doodling .... Drawing ...

Date _____

Day

I feel _____ this morning

Today's affirmation is _____

My ONE goal for today is _____

Accomplished? YES/NO

What can I do to make it better? ─────────────
_____

Today, I ate : a little/ enough/ too much

I happily drink : 🥛🥛🥛🥛🥛🥛🥛

What I did today

☐ Take My Shower   ☐ Exercise   ☐ Prayers

☐ Outdoor Activities   ☐ _____   ☐ _____

AT NIGHT

Today, I am grateful for _____

My mood today : ☆ ☆ ☆ ☆ ☆

Did I stay sober today?   YES / NO

My thoughts for today

_____
_____
_____

❝ When you forgive, you heal.
When you let go, you grow.
   - Anonymous ❞

Reflect .... Doodling ...... Drawing ...

Date _____    Day

I feel _____ this morning

Today's affirmation is _____

My ONE goal for today is _____

Accomplished? YES/NO

What can I do to make it better? ——————————————————

_____

Today, I ate : a little/ enough/ too much

I happily drink : 🥛🥛🥛🥛🥛🥛🥛

What I did today

☐ Take My Shower   ☐ Exercise   ☐ Prayers

☐ Outdoor Activities   ☐ _____   ☐ _____

AT NIGHT

Today, I am grateful for _____

My mood today : ☆ ☆ ☆ ☆ ☆

Did I stay sober today?   YES / NO

My thoughts for today

_____

_____

_____

❝ Yesterday is gone and its tale
told. Today new seeds are
growing - Rumi **❞**

Date _____

I feel _____ this morning

Today's affirmation is _____

My ONE goal for today is _____

Accomplished? YES/NO

What can I do to make it better? ———————————

_____

Today, I ate : a little/ enough/ too much

I happily drink : ▢▢▢▢▢▢▢

What I did today

▢ Take My Shower   ▢ Exercise   ▢ Prayers

▢ Outdoor Activities ▢ _____   ▢ _____

AT NIGHT

Today, I am grateful for _____

My mood today : ☆ ☆ ☆ ☆ ☆

Did I stay sober today?   YES / NO

My thoughts for today

_____

_____

_____

> To forgive is the highest, most
> beautiful form of love.
> In return, you will receive untold
> peace and happiness.
> - Robert Muller

Reflect .... Doodling ...... Drawing ...

Date _____  Day

I feel _____ this morning

Today's affirmation is _____

My ONE goal for today is _____

Accomplished? YES/NO

What can I do to make it better? _____

_____

Today, I ate : a little/ enough/ too much

I happily drink : 🥛🥛🥛🥛🥛🥛🥛

What I did today

☐ Take My Shower   ☐ Exercise   ☐ Prayers

☐ Outdoor Activities   ☐ _____   ☐ _____

AT NIGHT

Today, I am grateful for _____

My mood today : ☆ ☆ ☆ ☆ ☆

Did I stay sober today?   YES / NO

My thoughts for today

_____

_____

_____

Our greatest glory is not in never failing, but in rising up every time we fail.
- Ralph Waldo Emerson 99

Date _____

I feel _____ this morning

Today's affirmation is _____

My ONE goal for today is _____

Accomplished? YES/NO

What can I do to make it better? ―――――――――――――

_____

Today, I ate : a little/ enough/ too much

I happily drink : ⊔⊔⊔⊔⊔⊔⊔

What I did today

☐ Take My Shower   ☐ Exercise   ☐ Prayers

☐ Outdoor Activities   ☐ _____   ☐ _____

AT NIGHT

Today, I am grateful for _____

My mood today : ☆ ☆ ☆ ☆ ☆

Did I stay sober today?   YES / NO

My thoughts for today

_____

_____

_____

> Joy does not simply happen to us. We have to choose joy and keep choosing it every day.
> — Henri Nouwen

Reflect .... Doodling .... Drawing ....

Date _____

Day

I feel _____ this morning

Today's affirmation is _____

My ONE goal for today is _____

Accomplished? YES/NO

What can I do to make it better? _____
_____

Today, I ate : a little/ enough/ too much

I happily drink : ☐☐☐☐☐☐☐

What I did today

☐ Take My Shower   ☐ Exercise   ☐ Prayers

☐ Outdoor Activities ☐ _____   ☐ _____

AT NIGHT

Today, I am grateful for _____

My mood today : ☆ ☆ ☆ ☆ ☆

Did I stay sober today?   YES / NO

My thoughts for today

_____
_____
_____

66 Adopt the pace of nature; her
   secret is patience .
   - Ralph Waldo Enerson 99

....

....

....

....

....

....

....

....

....

....

....

....

....

....

....

....

Reflect .... Doodling .... Drawing ...

Date _____    Day

I feel _____ this morning

Today's affirmation is _____

My ONE goal for today is _____

Accomplished? YES/NO

What can I do to make it better? ——————————————

_____

Today, I ate : a little/ enough/ too much

I happily drink : 🥛🥛🥛🥛🥛🥛🥛

What I did today

☐ Take My Shower   ☐ Exercise   ☐ Prayers

☐ Outdoor Activities ☐ _____   ☐ _____

AT NIGHT

Today, I am grateful for _____

My mood today : ☆ ☆ ☆ ☆ ☆

Did I stay sober today?   YES / NO

My thoughts for today

_____

_____

_____

Reflect .... Doodling ...... Drawing ....

Date _____

Day

I feel _____ this morning

Today's affirmation is _____

My ONE goal for today is _____

Accomplished? YES/NO

What can I do to make it better? ——————————————

_____

Today, I ate : a little/ enough/ too much

I happily drink : ▨▨▨▨▨▨▨

What I did today

☐ Take My Shower   ☐ Exercise   ☐ Prayers

☐ Outdoor Activities   ☐ _____   ☐ _____

AT NIGHT

Today, I am grateful for _____

My mood today : ☆ ☆ ☆ ☆ ☆

Did I stay sober today?   YES / NO

My thoughts for today

_____

_____

_____

❝ Life often teaches us through
our wrong turns and missed
possibilities.
- Anne Wilson Schaef **❞**

Date _____

Day

I feel _____ this morning

Today's affirmation is _____

My ONE goal for today is _____

Accomplished? YES/NO

What can I do to make it better? ―――――――――――――

_____

Today, I ate : a little/ enough/ too much

I happily drink : 🥛🥛🥛🥛🥛🥛🥛

What I did today

☐ Take My Shower   ☐ Exercise   ☐ Prayers

☐ Outdoor Activities   ☐ _____   ☐ _____

AT NIGHT

Today, I am grateful for _____

My mood today : ☆ ☆ ☆ ☆ ☆

Did I stay sober today?   YES / NO

My thoughts for today

_____

_____

_____

It does not matter how
slowly you go as long as
you do not stop.
- Confucius

Reflect .... Doodling .... Drawing ...

Date _____

Day

I feel _____ this morning

Today's affirmation is _____

My ONE goal for today is _____

Accomplished? YES/NO

What can I do to make it better? ————————————————————

_____

Today, I ate : a little/ enough/ too much

I happily drink : 🥛🥛🥛🥛🥛🥛🥛

What I did today

☐ Take My Shower   ☐ Exercise   ☐ Prayers

☐ Outdoor Activities ☐ _____   ☐ _____

AT NIGHT

Today, I am grateful for _____

My mood today : ☆ ☆ ☆ ☆ ☆

Did I stay sober today?   YES / NO

My thoughts for today

_____

_____

_____

99 Learn from yesterday, live for
today, hope for tomorrow.
            - Albert Einstein   **99**

Reflect .... Doodling .... Drawing ....

....

....

....

....

....

....

....

....

....

....

....

....

....

....

....

....

Date _____

Day

I feel _____ this morning

Today's affirmation is _____

My ONE goal for today is _____

Accomplished? YES/NO

What can I do to make it better? ——————————

_____

Today, I ate : a little/ enough/ too much

I happily drink : ⬜⬜⬜⬜⬜⬜⬜

What I did today

☐ Take My Shower   ☐ Exercise   ☐ Prayers

☐ Outdoor Activities   ☐ _____   ☐ _____

AT NIGHT

Today, I am grateful for _____

My mood today : ☆ ☆ ☆ ☆ ☆

Did I stay sober today?   YES / NO

My thoughts for today

_____

_____

_____

❝❝ Nothing in this world is
impossible to a willing heart.
    - Abraham Lincoln   ❞❞

Reflect .... Doodling .... Drawing ....

Date _____    Day

I feel _____ this morning

Today's affirmation is _____

My ONE goal for today is _____

Accomplished? YES/NO

What can I do to make it better? _____

_____

Today, I ate : a little/ enough/ too much

I happily drink : 🥛🥛🥛🥛🥛🥛🥛

What I did today

☐ Take My Shower   ☐ Exercise   ☐ Prayers

☐ Outdoor Activities ☐ _____   ☐ _____

AT NIGHT

Today, I am grateful for _____

My mood today : ☆ ☆ ☆ ☆ ☆

Did I stay sober today?   YES / NO

My thoughts for today

_____

_____

_____

66 Everything gets better with time.
- Unknown 99

Date _____    Day

I feel _____ this morning

Today's affirmation is _____

My ONE goal for today is _____

Accomplished? YES/NO

What can I do to make it better? ——————————————————

_____

Today, I ate : a little/ enough/ too much

I happily drink : 🥛🥛🥛🥛🥛🥛🥛

What I did today

☐ Take My Shower   ☐ Exercise   ☐ Prayers

☐ Outdoor Activities   ☐ _____   ☐ _____

AT NIGHT

Today, I am grateful for _____

My mood today : ☆ ☆ ☆ ☆ ☆

Did I stay sober today?   YES / NO

My thoughts for today

_____

_____

_____

" When you forgive, you heal.
When you let go, you grow.
         - Anonymous **"**

Reflect .... Doodling ...... Drawing ....

Date _____

Day

I feel _____ this morning

Today's affirmation is _____

My ONE goal for today is _____

Accomplished? YES/NO

What can I do to make it better? ——————————

_____

Today, I ate : a little/ enough/ too much

I happily drink : 🥛🥛🥛🥛🥛🥛🥛

What I did today

☐ Take My Shower   ☐ Exercise   ☐ Prayers

☐ Outdoor Activities ☐ _____   ☐ _____

AT NIGHT

Today, I am grateful for _____

My mood today : ☆ ☆ ☆ ☆ ☆

Did I stay sober today?   YES / NO

My thoughts for today

_____

_____

_____

Yesterday is gone and its tale told. Today new seeds are growing - Rumi 💬

....

....

....

....

....

....

....

....

....

....

....

....

....

....

....

....

....

....

Date _____  Day

I feel _____ this morning

Today's affirmation is _____

My ONE goal for today is _____

Accomplished? YES/NO

What can I do to make it better? _____

_____

Today, I ate : a little/ enough/ too much

I happily drink : ▯▯▯▯▯▯▯

What I did today

☐ Take My Shower   ☐ Exercise   ☐ Prayers

☐ Outdoor Activities   ☐ _____   ☐ _____

AT NIGHT

Today, I am grateful for _____

My mood today : ☆ ☆ ☆ ☆ ☆

Did I stay sober today?   YES / NO

My thoughts for today

_____

_____

_____

> To forgive is the highest, most
> beautiful form of love.
> In return, you will receive untold
> peace and happiness.
> - Robert Muller

Reflect .... Doodling .... Drawing ....

Date _____

Day

I feel _____ this morning

Today's affirmation is _____

My ONE goal for today is _____

Accomplished? YES/NO

What can I do to make it better? ————————————

_____

Today, I ate : a little/ enough/ too much

I happily drink : 🥛🥛🥛🥛🥛🥛🥛

What I did today

☐ Take My Shower   ☐ Exercise   ☐ Prayers

☐ Outdoor Activities   ☐ _____   ☐ _____

AT NIGHT

Today, I am grateful for _____

My mood today : ☆ ☆ ☆ ☆ ☆

Did I stay sober today?   YES / NO

My thoughts for today

_____

_____

_____

> Our greatest glory is not in never failing, but in rising up every time we fail.
> - Ralph Waldo Emerson

Date _____  Day

I feel _____ this morning

Today's affirmation is _____

My ONE goal for today is _____

Accomplished? YES/NO

What can I do to make it better? ————————————————

_____

Today, I ate : a little/ enough/ too much

I happily drink : ▯▯▯▯▯▯▯

What I did today

☐ Take My Shower   ☐ Exercise   ☐ Prayers

☐ Outdoor Activities   ☐ _____   ☐ _____

AT NIGHT

Today, I am grateful for _____

My mood today : ☆ ☆ ☆ ☆ ☆

Did I stay sober today?   YES / NO

My thoughts for today

_____

_____

_____

"Joy does not simply happen to us. We have to choose joy and keep choosing it every day.
- Henri Nouwen "

Reflect .... Doodling .... Drawing ....

Date _____

Day

I feel _____ this morning

Today's affirmation is _____

My ONE goal for today is _____

Accomplished? YES/NO

What can I do to make it better? _____

_____

Today, I ate : a little/ enough/ too much

I happily drink : ▢▢▢▢▢▢▢

What I did today

☐ Take My Shower   ☐ Exercise   ☐ Prayers

☐ Outdoor Activities   ☐ _____   ☐ _____

AT NIGHT

Today, I am grateful for _____

My mood today : ☆ ☆ ☆ ☆ ☆

Did I stay sober today?   YES / NO

My thoughts for today

_____

_____

_____

> Adopt the pace of nature; her
> secret is patience .
> - Ralph Waldo Enerson

$\mathcal{D}ate$ _____

$\mathcal{D}ay$

I feel _____ this morning

Today's affirmation is _____

My ONE goal for today is _____

Accomplished? YES/NO

What can I do to make it better? _____

_____

Today, I ate : a little/ enough/ too much

I happily drink : 🥤🥤🥤🥤🥤🥤🥤

What I did today

☐ Take My Shower   ☐ Exercise   ☐ Prayers

☐ Outdoor Activities ☐ _____   ☐ _____

AT NIGHT

Today, I am grateful for _____

My mood today : ☆ ☆ ☆ ☆ ☆

Did I stay sober today?   YES / NO

My thoughts for today

_____

_____

_____

66

No one can make you feel
inferior without your consent.
- Eleanor Roosevelt

99

Reflect .... Doodling .... Drawing ....

Date _____

Day

I feel _____ this morning

Today's affirmation is _____

My ONE goal for today is _____

Accomplished? YES/NO

What can I do to make it better? _____
_____

Today, I ate : a little/ enough/ too much

I happily drink : ▯▯▯▯▯▯▯

What I did today

☐ Take My Shower   ☐ Exercise   ☐ Prayers

☐ Outdoor Activities   ☐ _____   ☐ _____

AT NIGHT

Today, I am grateful for _____

My mood today : ☆ ☆ ☆ ☆ ☆

Did I stay sober today?   YES / NO

My thoughts for today

_____

_____

_____

❝ Life often teaches us through
our wrong turns and missed
possibilities.
- Anne Wilson Schaef   **❞**

Date _____  Day

I feel _____ this morning

Today's affirmation is _____

My ONE goal for today is _____

Accomplished? YES/NO

What can I do to make it better? _____
_____

Today, I ate : a little/ enough/ too much

I happily drink : 🥛🥛🥛🥛🥛🥛🥛

What I did today

☐ Take My Shower   ☐ Exercise   ☐ Prayers

☐ Outdoor Activities   ☐ _____   ☐ _____

AT NIGHT

Today, I am grateful for _____

My mood today : ☆ ☆ ☆ ☆ ☆

Did I stay sober today?   YES / NO

My thoughts for today

_____
_____
_____

> **It does not matter how slowly you go as long as you do not stop.**
> - Confucius

Reflect .... Doodling ...... Drawing ...

Date _____

Day

I feel _____ this morning

Today's affirmation is _____

My ONE goal for today is _____

Accomplished? YES/NO

What can I do to make it better? _____

_____

Today, I ate : a little/ enough/ too much

I happily drink : ⬜⬜⬜⬜⬜⬜⬜

What I did today

☐ Take My Shower   ☐ Exercise   ☐ Prayers

☐ Outdoor Activities ☐ _____   ☐ _____

AT NIGHT

Today, I am grateful for _____

My mood today : ☆ ☆ ☆ ☆ ☆

Did I stay sober today?   YES / NO

My thoughts for today

_____

_____

_____

❝ Learn from yesterday, live for
today, hope for tomorrow.
       - Albert Einstein   **❞**

....

....

....

....

....

....

....

....

....

....

....

....

....

....

....

....

....

Date _____

Day

I feel _____ this morning

Today's affirmation is _____

My ONE goal for today is _____

Accomplished? YES/NO

What can I do to make it better? ─────────────

_____

Today, I ate : a little/ enough/ too much

I happily drink : ▯▯▯▯▯▯▯

What I did today

☐ Take My Shower   ☐ Exercise   ☐ Prayers

☐ Outdoor Activities ☐ _____ ☐ _____

AT NIGHT

Today, I am grateful for _____

My mood today : ☆ ☆ ☆ ☆ ☆

Did I stay sober today?   YES / NO

My thoughts for today

_____

_____

_____

66 Nothing in this world is
impossible to a willing heart.
- Abraham Lincoln 99

Reflect .... Doodling ...... Drawing ....

Date _____

Day

I feel _____ this morning

Today's affirmation is _____

My ONE goal for today is _____

Accomplished? YES/NO

What can I do to make it better? ———————————

_____

Today, I ate : a little/ enough/ too much

I happily drink : ▢▢▢▢▢▢▢

What I did today

☐ Take My Shower   ☐ Exercise   ☐ Prayers

☐ Outdoor Activities ☐ _____ ☐ _____

AT NIGHT

Today, I am grateful for _____

My mood today : ☆ ☆ ☆ ☆ ☆

Did I stay sober today?   YES / NO

My thoughts for today

_____

_____

_____

....

....

....

....

....

....

....

....

....

....

....

....

....

....

....

....

....

Date _____

Day

I feel _____ this morning

Today's affirmation is _____

My ONE goal for today is _____

Accomplished? YES/NO

What can I do to make it better? ———————————————

_____

Today, I ate : a little/ enough/ too much

I happily drink : ▢▢▢▢▢▢▢

What I did today

☐ Take My Shower   ☐ Exercise   ☐ Prayers

☐ Outdoor Activities ☐ _____   ☐ _____

AT NIGHT

Today, I am grateful for _____

My mood today : ☆ ☆ ☆ ☆ ☆

Did I stay sober today?   YES / NO

My thoughts for today

_____

_____

_____

" When you forgive, you heal.
When you let go, you grow.
- Anonymous **"**

Reflect .... Doodling ...... Drawing ....

Date _____

I feel _____ this morning

Today's affirmation is _____

My ONE goal for today is _____

Accomplished? YES/NO

What can I do to make it better? ———————————————

_____

Today, I ate : a little/ enough/ too much

I happily drink : ⊞⊞⊞⊞⊞⊞⊞

┌───┐
│   What I did today   │
│ ☐ Take My Shower   ☐ Exercise   ☐ Prayers │
│ ☐ Outdoor Activities ☐ _____   ☐ _____ │
└───┘

AT NIGHT

Today, I am grateful for _____

My mood today : ☆ ☆ ☆ ☆ ☆

Did I stay sober today?   YES / NO

┌───┐
│   My thoughts for today   │
│ _____ │
│ _____ │
│ _____ │
└───┘

> Yesterday is gone and its tale told. Today new seeds are growing - Rumi

Reflect .... Doodling ...... Drawing ....

Date _____

I feel _____ this morning

Today's affirmation is _____

My ONE goal for today is _____

Accomplished? YES/NO

What can I do to make it better? ─────────────

_____

Today, I ate : a little/ enough/ too much

I happily drink : 🥛🥛🥛🥛🥛🥛🥛

What I did today		
☐ Take My Shower	☐ Exercise	☐ Prayers
☐ Outdoor Activities	☐ _____	☐ _____

AT NIGHT

Today, I am grateful for _____

My mood today : ☆ ☆ ☆ ☆ ☆

Did I stay sober today?   YES / NO

My thoughts for today
_____
_____
_____

❝ To forgive is the highest, most
beautiful form of love.
In return, you will receive untold
peace and happiness.
- Robert Muller **❞**

Reflect .... Doodling .... Drawing ....

Date _____

Day

I feel _____ this morning

Today's affirmation is _____

My ONE goal for today is _____

Accomplished? YES/NO

What can I do to make it better? _____

_____

Today, I ate : a little/ enough/ too much

I happily drink : 🥛🥛🥛🥛🥛🥛🥛

What I did today

☐ Take My Shower   ☐ Exercise   ☐ Prayers

☐ Outdoor Activities   ☐ _____   ☐ _____

AT NIGHT

Today, I am grateful for _____

My mood today : ☆ ☆ ☆ ☆ ☆

Did I stay sober today?   YES / NO

My thoughts for today

_____

_____

_____

❝ Our greatest glory is not in never
failing, but in rising up every
time we fail.
- Ralph Waldo Emerson **❞**

···
···
···
···
···
···
···
···
···
···
···
···
···
···
···
···
···

$\mathcal{Date}$ _____  $\mathcal{Day}$

I feel _____ this morning

Today's affirmation is _____

My ONE goal for today is _____

Accomplished? YES/NO

What can I do to make it better? _____

_____

Today, I ate : a little/ enough/ too much

I happily drink : ⊞⊞⊞⊞⊞⊞⊞

What I did today

☐ Take My Shower   ☐ Exercise   ☐ Prayers

☐ Outdoor Activities   ☐ _____   ☐ _____

AT NIGHT

Today, I am grateful for _____

My mood today : ☆ ☆ ☆ ☆ ☆

Did I stay sober today?   YES / NO

My thoughts for today

_____

_____

_____

> Joy does not simply happen to us. We have to choose joy and keep choosing it every day.
>
> - Henri Nouwen

Reflect .... Doodling ...... Drawing ...

Date _____  Day

I feel _____ this morning

Today's affirmation is _____

My ONE goal for today is _____

Accomplished? YES/NO

What can I do to make it better? ——————————————

_____

Today, I ate : a little/ enough/ too much

I happily drink : ▯▯▯▯▯▯▯

What I did today

☐ Take My Shower   ☐ Exercise   ☐ Prayers

☐ Outdoor Activities   ☐ _____   ☐ _____

AT NIGHT

Today, I am grateful for _____

My mood today : ☆ ☆ ☆ ☆ ☆

Did I stay sober today?   YES / NO

My thoughts for today

_____

_____

_____

❝❝ Adopt the pace of nature; her
    secret is patience .
    - Ralph Waldo Enerson ❞❞

Reflect .... Doodling .... Drawing ....

Date _____

I feel _____ this morning

Today's affirmation is _____

My ONE goal for today is _____

Accomplished? YES/NO

What can I do to make it better? ————————————————

_____

Today, I ate : a little/ enough/ too much

I happily drink : ▯▯▯▯▯▯▯

What I did today

☐ Take My Shower   ☐ Exercise   ☐ Prayers

☐ Outdoor Activities   ☐ _____   ☐ _____

AT NIGHT

Today, I am grateful for _____

My mood today : ☆ ☆ ☆ ☆ ☆

Did I stay sober today?   YES / NO

My thoughts for today

_____

_____

_____

❝❝ No one can make you feel
inferior without your consent.
- Eleanor Roosevelt ❞❞

Reflect .... Doodling ...... Drawing ...

$\mathcal{D}ate$ _____

$\mathcal{D}ay$

I feel _____ this morning

Today's affirmation is _____

My ONE goal for today is _____

Accomplished? YES/NO

What can I do to make it better? ―――――――――――――――――

_____

Today, I ate : a little/ enough/ too much

I happily drink : ▯▯▯▯▯▯▯

What I did today

☐ Take My Shower   ☐ Exercise   ☐ Prayers

☐ Outdoor Activities   ☐ _____   ☐ _____

AT NIGHT

Today, I am grateful for _____

My mood today : ☆ ☆ ☆ ☆ ☆

Did I stay sober today?   YES / NO

My thoughts for today

_____

_____

_____

> Life often teaches us through
> our wrong turns and missed
> possibilities.
> - Anne Wilson Schaef

Date _____

Day

I feel _____ this morning

Today's affirmation is _____

My ONE goal for today is _____

Accomplished? YES/NO

What can I do to make it better? _____

_____

Today, I ate : a little/ enough/ too much

I happily drink : ▢▢▢▢▢▢▢

What I did today

☐ Take My Shower   ☐ Exercise   ☐ Prayers

☐ Outdoor Activities ☐ _____   ☐ _____

AT NIGHT

Today, I am grateful for _____

My mood today : ☆ ☆ ☆ ☆ ☆

Did I stay sober today?   YES / NO

My thoughts for today

_____

_____

_____

" It does not matter how
slowly you go as long as
you do not stop.
- Confucius **"**

Reflect .... Doodling .... Drawing ...

Date _____ Day

I feel _____ this morning

Today's affirmation is _____

My ONE goal for today is _____

Accomplished? YES/NO

What can I do to make it better? ———————————

_____

Today, I ate : a little/ enough/ too much

I happily drink : 🥛🥛🥛🥛🥛🥛🥛

What I did today

☐ Take My Shower   ☐ Exercise   ☐ Prayers

☐ Outdoor Activities   ☐ _____   ☐ _____

AT NIGHT

Today, I am grateful for _____

My mood today : ☆ ☆ ☆ ☆ ☆

Did I stay sober today?   YES / NO

My thoughts for today

_____

_____

_____

“ Learn from yesterday, live for
today, hope for tomorrow.
  - Albert Einstein ”

Date _____

I feel _____ this morning

Today's affirmation is _____

My ONE goal for today is _____

Accomplished? YES/NO

What can I do to make it better? ———————————

_____

Today, I ate : a little/ enough/ too much

I happily drink : ▯▯▯▯▯▯▯

What I did today

☐ Take My Shower   ☐ Exercise   ☐ Prayers

☐ Outdoor Activities   ☐ _____   ☐ _____

AT NIGHT

Today, I am grateful for _____

My mood today : ☆ ☆ ☆ ☆ ☆

Did I stay sober today?   YES / NO

My thoughts for today

_____

_____

_____

" Nothing in this world is
impossible to a willing heart.
    - Abraham Lincoln "

Date _____

Day

I feel _____ this morning

Today's affirmation is _____

My ONE goal for today is _____

Accomplished? YES/NO

What can I do to make it better? —————————————

_____

Today, I ate : a little/ enough/ too much

I happily drink : 🥃🥃🥃🥃🥃🥃🥃

What I did today

☐ Take My Shower   ☐ Exercise   ☐ Prayers

☐ Outdoor Activities ☐ _____ ☐ _____

AT NIGHT

Today, I am grateful for _____

My mood today : ☆ ☆ ☆ ☆ ☆

Did I stay sober today?   YES / NO

My thoughts for today

_____

_____

_____

" Everything gets better with time.
- Unknown **"**

Date _____

I feel _____ this morning

Today's affirmation is _____

My ONE goal for today is _____

Accomplished? YES/NO

What can I do to make it better? _____

_____

Today, I ate : a little/ enough/ too much

I happily drink : ▢▢▢▢▢▢▢

What I did today

☐ Take My Shower   ☐ Exercise   ☐ Prayers

☐ Outdoor Activities   ☐ _____   ☐ _____

AT NIGHT

Today, I am grateful for _____

My mood today : ☆ ☆ ☆ ☆ ☆

Did I stay sober today?   YES / NO

My thoughts for today

_____

_____

_____

" When you forgive, you heal.
When you let go, you grow.
      - Anonymous   **"**

Reflect .... Doodling .... Drawing ....

Date _____    *Day*

I feel _____ this morning

Today's affirmation is _____

My ONE goal for today is _____

Accomplished? YES/NO

What can I do to make it better? ——————————————

_____

Today, I ate : a little/ enough/ too much

I happily drink : 🥛🥛🥛🥛🥛🥛🥛

What I did today

☐ Take My Shower   ☐ Exercise   ☐ Prayers

☐ Outdoor Activities   ☐ _____   ☐ _____

AT NIGHT

Today, I am grateful for _____

My mood today : ☆ ☆ ☆ ☆ ☆

Did I stay sober today?   YES / NO

My thoughts for today

_____

_____

_____

Yesterday is gone and its tale
told. Today new seeds are
growing - Rumi

Reflect .... Doodling .... Drawing ....

Date _____

Day

I feel _____ this morning

Today's affirmation is _____

My ONE goal for today is _____

Accomplished? YES/NO

What can I do to make it better? ——————————————

_____

Today, I ate : a little/ enough/ too much

I happily drink : ▢▢▢▢▢▢▢▢

What I did today

☐ Take My Shower   ☐ Exercise   ☐ Prayers

☐ Outdoor Activities   ☐ _____   ☐ _____

AT NIGHT

Today, I am grateful for _____

My mood today : ☆ ☆ ☆ ☆ ☆

Did I stay sober today?   YES / NO

My thoughts for today

_____

_____

_____

To forgive is the highest, most
beautiful form of love.
In return, you will receive untold
peace and happiness.
- Robert Muller

Reflect .... Doodling .... Drawing ...

Date _____

Day

I feel _____ this morning

Today's affirmation is _____

My ONE goal for today is _____

Accomplished? YES/NO

What can I do to make it better? —————————————

_____

Today, I ate : a little/ enough/ too much

I happily drink : 🥛🥛🥛🥛🥛🥛🥛

What I did today

☐ Take My Shower   ☐ Exercise   ☐ Prayers

☐ Outdoor Activities   ☐ _____   ☐ _____

AT NIGHT

Today, I am grateful for _____

My mood today : ☆ ☆ ☆ ☆ ☆

Did I stay sober today?   YES / NO

My thoughts for today

_____

_____

_____

> Our greatest glory is not in never failing, but in rising up every time we fail.
> - Ralph Waldo Emerson

Date _____

Day

I feel _____ this morning

Today's affirmation is _____

My ONE goal for today is _____

Accomplished? YES/NO

What can I do to make it better? ————————————————

_____

Today, I ate : a little/ enough/ too much

I happily drink : ▢▢▢▢▢▢▢

What I did today

☐ Take My Shower   ☐ Exercise   ☐ Prayers

☐ Outdoor Activities   ☐ _____   ☐ _____

AT NIGHT

Today, I am grateful for _____

My mood today : ☆ ☆ ☆ ☆ ☆

Did I stay sober today?   YES / NO

My thoughts for today

_____

_____

_____

66 Joy does not simply happen to
us. We have to choose joy and
keep choosing it every day.
    - Henri Nouwen   99

Date _____

Day

I feel _____ this morning

Today's affirmation is _____

My ONE goal for today is _____

Accomplished? YES/NO

What can I do to make it better? ─────────────────

_____

Today, I ate : a little/ enough/ too much

I happily drink : 🥛🥛🥛🥛🥛🥛🥛

What I did today

☐ Take My Shower   ☐ Exercise   ☐ Prayers

☐ Outdoor Activities   ☐ _____   ☐ _____

AT NIGHT

Today, I am grateful for _____

My mood today : ☆ ☆ ☆ ☆ ☆

Did I stay sober today?   YES / NO

My thoughts for today

_____

_____

_____

66 Adopt the pace of nature; her
          secret is patience .
          - Ralph Waldo Enerson   99

Reflect .... Doodling .... Drawing ...

$\mathcal{D}ate$ _____

$\mathcal{D}ay$

I feel _____this morning

Today's affirmation is _____

My ONE goal for today is _____

Accomplished? YES/NO

What can I do to make it better? _____

_____

Today, I ate : a little/ enough/ too much

I happily drink : 🥛🥛🥛🥛🥛🥛🥛

What I did today

☐ Take My Shower   ☐ Exercise   ☐ Prayers

☐ Outdoor Activities   ☐ _____   ☐ _____

AT NIGHT

Today, I am grateful for _____

My mood today : ☆ ☆ ☆ ☆ ☆

Did I stay sober today?   YES / NO

My thoughts for today

_____

_____

_____

" No one can make you feel
inferior without your consent.
- Eleanor Roosevelt **"**

Reflect .... Doodling .... Drawing ....

Date _____

Day

I feel _____ this morning

Today's affirmation is _____

My ONE goal for today is _____

Accomplished? YES/NO

What can I do to make it better? _____

_____

Today, I ate : a little/ enough/ too much

I happily drink : ⊟ ⊟ ⊟ ⊟ ⊟ ⊟ ⊟

What I did today

☐ Take My Shower   ☐ Exercise   ☐ Prayers

☐ Outdoor Activities ☐ _____   ☐ _____

AT NIGHT

Today, I am grateful for _____

My mood today : ☆ ☆ ☆ ☆ ☆

Did I stay sober today?   YES / NO

My thoughts for today

_____

_____

_____

" Life often teaches us through
our wrong turns and missed
possibilities.
- Anne Wilson Schaef **"**

Reflect .... Doodling .... Drawing ....

Date _____

I feel _____ this morning

Today's affirmation is _____

My ONE goal for today is _____

Accomplished? YES/NO

What can I do to make it better? ——————————

_____

Today, I ate : a little/ enough/ too much

I happily drink : ▢▢▢▢▢▢▢

What I did today

☐ Take My Shower   ☐ Exercise   ☐ Prayers

☐ Outdoor Activities   ☐ _____   ☐ _____

AT NIGHT

Today, I am grateful for _____

My mood today : ☆ ☆ ☆ ☆ ☆

Did I stay sober today?   YES / NO

My thoughts for today

_____

_____

_____

> **It does not matter how slowly you go as long as you do not stop.**
> - Confucius

Reflect .... Doodling ...... Drawing ....

Date _____

Day

I feel _____ this morning

Today's affirmation is _____

My ONE goal for today is _____

Accomplished? YES/NO

What can I do to make it better? ──────────────

_____

Today, I ate : a little/ enough/ too much

I happily drink : 🥛🥛🥛🥛🥛🥛🥛

What I did today

☐ Take My Shower   ☐ Exercise   ☐ Prayers

☐ Outdoor Activities   ☐ _____   ☐ _____

AT NIGHT

Today, I am grateful for _____

My mood today : ☆ ☆ ☆ ☆ ☆

Did I stay sober today?   YES / NO

My thoughts for today

_____

_____

_____

Learn from yesterday, live for
today, hope for tomorrow.
- Albert Einstein

Date _____

Day

I feel _____ this morning

Today's affirmation is _____

My ONE goal for today is _____

Accomplished? YES/NO

What can I do to make it better? ————————————

_____

Today, I ate : a little/ enough/ too much

I happily drink : ⊟⊟⊟⊟⊟⊟⊟

What I did today

☐ Take My Shower ☐ Exercise ☐ Prayers

☐ Outdoor Activities ☐ _____ ☐ _____

AT NIGHT

Today, I am grateful for _____

My mood today : ☆ ☆ ☆ ☆ ☆

Did I stay sober today?   YES / NO

My thoughts for today

_____

_____

_____

"

Nothing in this world is
impossible to a willing heart.
- Abraham Lincoln "

Reflect .... Doodling ...... Drawing ...

Date _____

I feel _____ this morning

Today's affirmation is _____

My ONE goal for today is _____

Accomplished? YES/NO

What can I do to make it better? ——————————

_____

Today, I ate : a little/ enough/ too much

I happily drink : 🥛🥛🥛🥛🥛🥛🥛

What I did today

☐ Take My Shower   ☐ Exercise   ☐ Prayers

☐ Outdoor Activities ☐ _____   ☐ _____

AT NIGHT

Today, I am grateful for _____

My mood today : ☆ ☆ ☆ ☆ ☆

Did I stay sober today?   YES / NO

My thoughts for today

_____

_____

_____

> Everything gets better with time.
> - Unknown

Date _____

Day

I feel _____ this morning

Today's affirmation is _____

My ONE goal for today is _____

Accomplished? YES/NO

What can I do to make it better? ————————————

_____

Today, I ate : a little/ enough/ too much

I happily drink : 🥛🥛🥛🥛🥛🥛🥛

What I did today

☐ Take My Shower ☐ Exercise ☐ Prayers

☐ Outdoor Activities ☐ _____ ☐ _____

AT NIGHT

Today, I am grateful for _____

My mood today : ☆ ☆ ☆ ☆ ☆

Did I stay sober today?   YES / NO

My thoughts for today

_____

_____

_____

When you forgive, you heal.
When you let go, you grow.
- Anonymous

Reflect .... Doodling .... Drawing ....

Date _____

I feel _____ this morning

Today's affirmation is _____

My ONE goal for today is _____

Accomplished? YES/NO

What can I do to make it better? ————————————

_____

Today, I ate : a little/ enough/ too much

I happily drink : 🥛🥛🥛🥛🥛🥛🥛

What I did today

☐ Take My Shower   ☐ Exercise   ☐ Prayers

☐ Outdoor Activities   ☐ _____   ☐ _____

AT NIGHT

Today, I am grateful for _____

My mood today : ☆ ☆ ☆ ☆ ☆

Did I stay sober today?   YES / NO

My thoughts for today

_____

_____

_____

❝ Yesterday is gone and its tale told. Today new seeds are growing - Rumi **❞**

Reflect .... Doodling .... Drawing ....

Date _____

I feel _____ this morning

Today's affirmation is _____

My ONE goal for today is _____

Accomplished? YES/NO

What can I do to make it better? ——————————————————

_____

Today, I ate : a little/ enough/ too much

I happily drink : 🥛🥛🥛🥛🥛🥛🥛

What I did today

☐ Take My Shower   ☐ Exercise   ☐ Prayers

☐ Outdoor Activities ☐ _____   ☐ _____

AT NIGHT

Today, I am grateful for _____

My mood today : ☆ ☆ ☆ ☆ ☆

Did I stay sober today?   YES / NO

My thoughts for today

_____

_____

_____

To forgive is the highest, most
beautiful form of love.
In return, you will receive untold
peace and happiness.
- Robert Muller

Reflect .... Doodling .... Drawing ....

Date _____

Day

I feel _____ this morning

Today's affirmation is _____

My ONE goal for today is _____

Accomplished? YES/NO

What can I do to make it better? ─────────────────────

_____

Today, I ate : a little/ enough/ too much

I happily drink : 🥛🥛🥛🥛🥛🥛🥛

What I did today

☐ Take My Shower   ☐ Exercise   ☐ Prayers

☐ Outdoor Activities   ☐ _____   ☐ _____

AT NIGHT

Today, I am grateful for _____

My mood today : ☆ ☆ ☆ ☆ ☆

Did I stay sober today?   YES / NO

My thoughts for today

_____

_____

_____

" Our greatest glory is not in never
failing, but in rising up every
time we fail.
- Ralph Waldo Emerson "

Reflect .... Doodling ...... Drawing ...

Date _____    Day

I feel _____ this morning

Today's affirmation is _____

My ONE goal for today is _____

Accomplished? YES/NO

What can I do to make it better? ─────────────────

_____

Today, I ate : a little/ enough/ too much

I happily drink : 🥛🥛🥛🥛🥛🥛🥛

What I did today

☐ Take My Shower   ☐ Exercise   ☐ Prayers

☐ Outdoor Activities   ☐ _____   ☐ _____

AT NIGHT

Today, I am grateful for _____

My mood today : ☆ ☆ ☆ ☆ ☆

Did I stay sober today?   YES / NO

My thoughts for today

_____

_____

_____

" Joy does not simply happen to us. We have to choose joy and keep choosing it every day.
- Henri Nouwen "

Date _____  Day

I feel _____ this morning

Today's affirmation is _____

My ONE goal for today is _____

Accomplished? YES/NO

What can I do to make it better? ————————————————

_____

Today, I ate : a little/ enough/ too much

I happily drink : ▯ ▯ ▯ ▯ ▯ ▯ ▯

What I did today

☐ Take My Shower   ☐ Exercise   ☐ Prayers

☐ Outdoor Activities   ☐ _____   ☐ _____

AT NIGHT

Today, I am grateful for _____

My mood today : ☆ ☆ ☆ ☆ ☆

Did I stay sober today?   YES / NO

My thoughts for today

_____

_____

_____

“ Adopt the pace of nature; her
secret is patience .
- Ralph Waldo Enerson ”

Made in United States
Troutdale, OR
05/09/2024

19742568R00106